W9-BLP-330

Pain Treatments

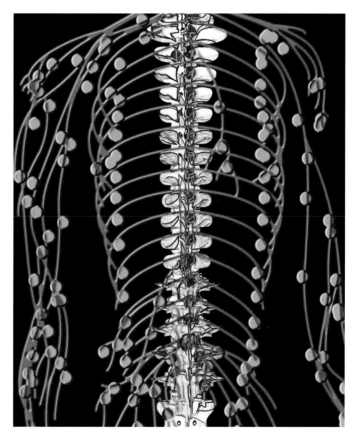

L. H. Colligan

Cavendish Square

New York

Title page: Nerve endings carry pain signals to and from the brain.

Special thanks to Adam J. Adler of the University of Connecticut Health Center for his expert review of this manuscript.

Published in 2014 by Cavendish Square Publishing, LLC
303 Park Avenue South, Suite 1247, New York, NY 10010

Library of Congress Cataloging-in-Publication Data
Colligan, L. H.
Pain treatments / L.H. Colligan.
p. cm. – (Advances in medicine)
Includes bibliographical references and index.
Summary: "Discusses the advances that have been made in treating pain"–Provided by publisher.
ISBN 978-1-60870-468-2 (hardcover) ISBN 978-1-62712-011-1 (paperback) 978-1-60870-596-2 (ebook)
1. Pain–Treatment–Juvenile literature. I. Title.
RB127.C63 2012
616'.0472–dc22
2010042492

Editor: Megan Comerford
Art Director: Anahid Hamparian   Series Designer: Nancy Sabato

Photo research by Edward Thomas
Front cover photo by Getty Images: Dale O'Dell - Stock Connection
Back cover photo and chapter openers by Dreamstime

The photographs in this book are used by permission and through the courtesy of: *Alamy*: © Dellnesco, 25; © Dave Zubraski, 27; © Bill Watson, 29; © Blend Images, 35; © Enigma, 40; © Ira Weiny, 51. *Getty Images*: SSPL, 32. *Glow Images*: © Rick Gomez/Corbis, 18. © Hunter Hoffman, UW, www.vrpain.com, 49. Newscom: Gerry Melendez/ The State/MCT, 17. *Photo Researchers*, Inc.: Apogee, 4; PClaus Lunau / Bonnier Publications, 36; Carolyn A. McKeone, 46. *StockphotoPro*: Joubert, 1, 11. *Superstock*: © Stockbroker, 7; © Corbis, 8.

Printed in the United States of America

contents

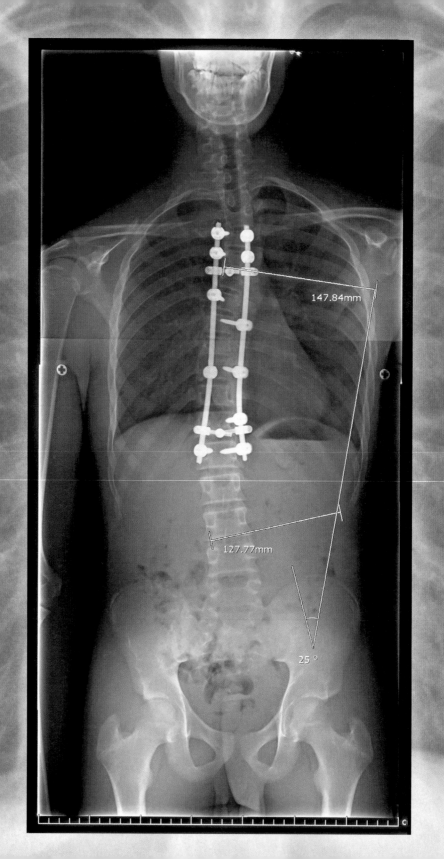

chapter 1

What Is It Like to Have Pain Treatments?

Nobody ever tells Hannah to stand up straight for a photograph. This high school sophomore with perfect posture got it the hard way. "In sixth grade I flunked my spinal test during a scoliosis screening at school," Hannah explains. "When the nurse checked my back, she saw that my spine was curving when it should have been straight. And my homework was having to go through an operation to put metal rods in my back!"

Pain medications and physical therapy can provide relief after an operation, such as the scoliosis surgery performed to implant spine-straightening metal rods as shown here.

Hannah jokes about her operation now that her back is nice and straight again. However, at the time, she was pretty scared. Doctors told her that the operation would take six hours and that she would be hospitalized for about a week. Afterward, they said, Hannah would need many weeks of **physical therapy** to get moving normally again.

Hannah thought of herself as being pretty tough. But she worried about **pain**. She was relieved to learn that she would follow a program of different pain treatments. "Thank goodness for the painkillers they gave me," Hannah says now. "I don't know how I would have gotten through my scoliosis surgery and healing without them."

One of the doctors present during the operation was an anesthesiologist, a doctor who specializes in pain medication. Hannah received a general **anesthesia** in the form of a gas that put her whole body to sleep before the operation. The anesthesia blocked all of Hannah's senses, so she felt no pain during the surgery.

That changed as soon as the anesthesia wore off after the surgery was over. Hannah woke up in the recovery room. She had no memory at all of her surgery, but she was very uncomfortable. She had to lie totally still. She also needed a breathing machine a few times a day to get her breathing back to normal.

"I have to admit, the pain was horrible at first," Hannah remembers. "I needed painkillers for the first few days. The great thing, though, was that I could control the amount of pain medication I needed through a special electronic pump! The doctors showed me how to use it. It is called a PCA, or patient-controlled analgesia. All I had to do was press a button. The pump released

Physical therapy improves muscle tone and heart and lung rates, and promotes healing that relieves pain symptoms.

strong **morphine** pain medication right through a tube going into my spine. I know that sounds gross, but the PCA really helped me so much those first few days when the pain was the worst."

After that, Hannah took milder kinds of pain medications in pill form. The pills were a combination of **acetaminophen** and **codeine**.

"I only needed those pills for a few weeks," Hannah remembers. "What helped me most were my physical therapy sessions. My therapist warmed up my muscles and then had me stretch and walk little by little. I did a lot of the same exercises at home, too. My mom gave me massages on my arms and legs. I listened to my music to stay calm. I rested, read a ton of books, and even learned how to knit. Those were the best painkillers of all. Now I've gone back to being the old me. If I get a headache or muscle ache, I apply an ice pack, take a rest, and the pain seems to go away by itself."

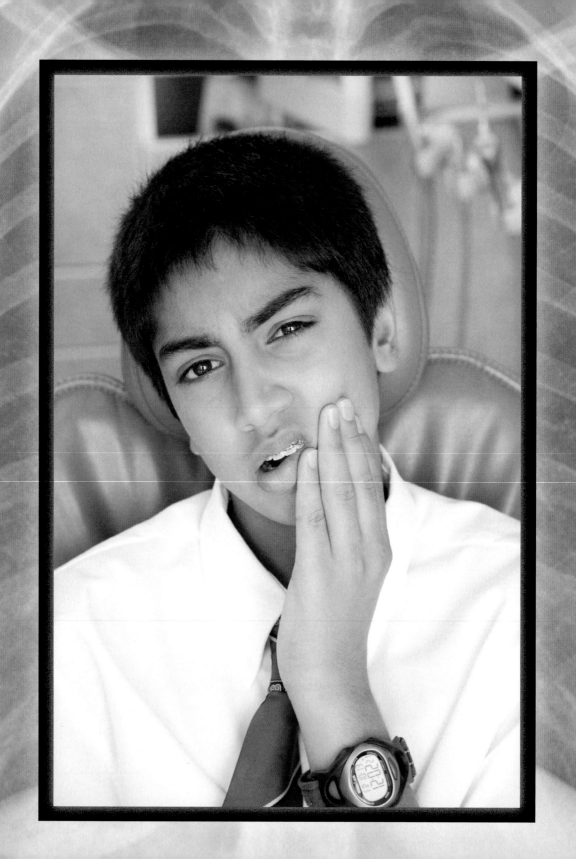

chapter 2

What Is Pain?

Pain is the awareness that something has gone wrong in the body. When we experience sudden, **acute pain**, such as a burn, a blow, a cut, or a cramp, we often cry out "Ouch!" or "Ow!" Most languages have short, single words to say "I'm hurt!" In Brazil it is "*Ai!*" In Spain it is "*Ay!*" German speakers say "*Autsch!*" These are cries for help and relief. People who suffer long-lasting **chronic pain**, such as an ongoing backache or joint pain from adult or juvenile rheumatoid **arthritis**, may moan and groan. Or they may not say anything at all. Instead, their muscles may tense up. They may

◄ Pain signals are a major alert that an injury needs attention.

frown and look fearful. They just want the hurt to stop. When we are in pain, we find it hard to focus, study, work, or enjoy regular everyday life even in pleasant situations.

But what if our bodies never experienced pain? A pain-free world would be great, right? Wrong. Pain messages teach us how to stay safe and healthy. They warn us to stop what we were doing when we hurt ourselves so we do not suffer further damage. Pain also affects the brain's memory centers. Pain memories help us to watch out for future dangers: hot, freezing, sharp, germ-covered, or dangerous objects; strange foods; harmful animals and insects; unfamiliar plants; steep heights; and more. So although pain hurts, we need it to survive.

How Does Pain Work?

Pain works by sending signals from injured parts of the body to the brain. The pain may begin in different areas and have different causes. No matter where pain starts, two major systems in the body coordinate in order to handle it: the **peripheral nervous system** and the **central nervous system**.

Peripheral Nervous System

At the moment of an injury, a pain-causing event, or an **infection**, the peripheral nervous system (PNS) kicks in first. This network of tiny **nerve cells** branches out from skin, bones, muscles, joints, organs, arms, and legs and connects to the **spinal cord**. Poisons, injuries, and infections directly harm PNS cells. Some nerve endings in these cells are sensitive to temperature and pressure. Other PNS nerve endings, called **nociceptors**, recognize forces likely to damage cell **tissues**.

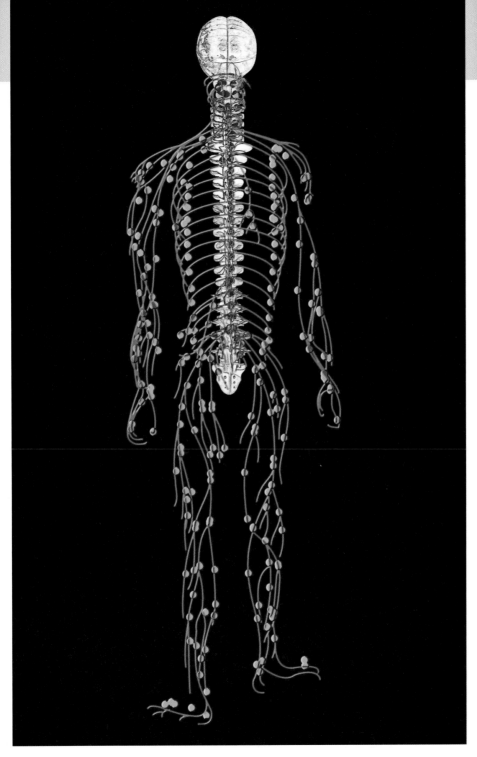

Nerve endings along the peripheral and central nervous systems carry
pain signals to and from the brain.

The Central Nervous System

You can think of the central nervous system (CNS) as the body's 911 call center. It is made up of the brain and spinal cord. The central nervous system is where pain messages quickly arrive after an injury or medical event happens in the peripheral nervous system. Pain messaging between both systems takes place fast. It is as if you called 911 and a fire truck, police car, and ambulance showed up as soon as you told the operator you were hurt.

Here is what happens in the first moments after an injury or medical event:

- Damaged cells at the injury site in the peripheral nervous system release a chemical messenger called **prostaglandin**.

- Nerve endings become sensitive to prostaglandin. *Something is hurt!*

- Prostaglandin also causes blood vessels to expand. When they do, the heart sends more blood to the injury site. This causes **inflammation**—the hot painful redness, swelling, and bruising you feel after you get hurt.

- The spinal cord releases its own chemical messengers called **neurotransmitters** to other spinal cord nerve cells and then on to the brain. When pain messages reach the brain, the brain responds in several ways.

- One reaction determines what the injury is, where it is located, and how severe it is. *The left shinbone was smashed below the front of the knee!*

- Another response triggers an emotional reaction—fear and stress—and involves memory centers. *Ouch, that hurts! I need to remember to wear shin guards next time!*

Another brain reaction sometimes signals the spinal cord to increase pain messages so that the injured person will take major protective actions. *Stop playing right now!*

The brain also causes the release of the body's own natural painkillers. These temporarily dull some of the pain messages so that the pain sufferer can cope with the injury.

The brain itself does not experience pain because it does not have pain receptors. This makes it possible for the brain to focus on sending help to the injury site.

How Much Does It Hurt?

Did you ever wonder if a pain you felt would feel the same to someone else? Pain researchers have wondered that, too. Thanks to **magnetic resonance imaging (MRI)** machines, pain experts can now study whether all pain sufferers experience pain the same way. It turns out they do not. Your pain experience may be different from your friend's.

In 2003 researchers at Wake Forest University in Winston-Salem, North Carolina, looked inside the brains of seventeen volunteers who agreed to have heat applied to their skin. These subjects then rated the pain from one to ten. Results showed that people who reported higher pain levels experienced more activity in certain parts of the brain than those who gave their pain lower ratings.

Until this important study was done, doctors were not always sure about how accurately people reported pain levels. It turns out that some people just feel more pain than others, especially in the part of the brain that deals with

RED ALERT

For years, some dentists and anesthesiologists had noticed something unusual going on with some of their redheaded patients. Many of them seemed to experience more pain and needed more pain medication than patients with other hair colors. Not only had dentists noticed that some of their redheaded patients avoided appointments, but many of these redheads seemed to have more fears about dental procedures, too.

What was it about redheads that seemed to make them fear pain and experience more of it than other patients? Dentists and pain experts at the American Dental Association (ADA) decided to find out. In 2009 the ADA enrolled 144 people between the ages of eighteen and forty-one in a dental pain study. Sixty-seven of them were natural redheads. The others were dark haired. Everyone filled out questionnaires about dental fears and whether they avoided dental visits. The ADA researchers also tested the blood of all the participants. They looked for differences in certain kinds of **genes** associated with both hair color and pain **receptors**.

The ADA study confirmed what many pain medication experts had noticed all along. Blood samples of sixty-five of the sixty-seven redheads showed differences in a certain gene called MC1R. These redheads expressed nearly double the worry and dental avoidance that the dark-haired subjects did. (Only twenty out of seventy-seven dark-haired subjects expressed strong fear of dental procedures.) Not only that, the ADA study confirmed an earlier 2004 study that found that many redheads needed about 20 percent more pain medication before surgery than most patients with dark or blond hair. A 2005 study showed that redheads were more resistant to numbing dental pain medication.

So what is an affected redhead to do? As they say in the television commercials, "Talk to your doctor or dentist." Specifically, ask if he or she is familiar with the dental and surgical studies that show red hair is not just about hair color on the outside but about a gene that may make redheads likely to feel more pain than most other patients.

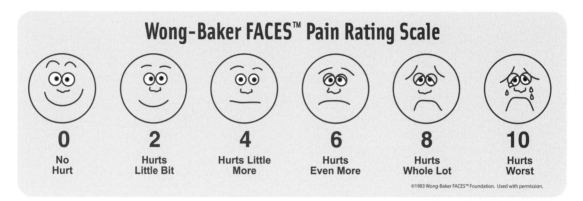

This pain scale helps patients rate their pain levels so that a doctor can appropriately diagnose and treat the problem. It was designed by the Wong-Baker FACES Foundation, an organization created to better understand and manage pain.

pain and emotions. This may be due to past pain memories, feelings at the time of the injury, or pain expectations. The lead researcher, Robert C. Coghill, believes that patients' "self-reports should guide treatment of pain."

Children and Pain

Guess who experiences the most pain of any age group? Kids do, especially those between the ages of nine and thirteen. A major 2007 Canadian study of childhood pain found that 96 percent of children experienced some kind of pain during the course of a particular month. A much lower percentage of adults reported experiencing pain for the same time period. It seems that adults, since they are not as active as children, do not suffer as many injuries as children do. Among the children, the study showed that boys had more bee stings and accidents requiring stitches, while girls had more earaches, toothaches, and burns.

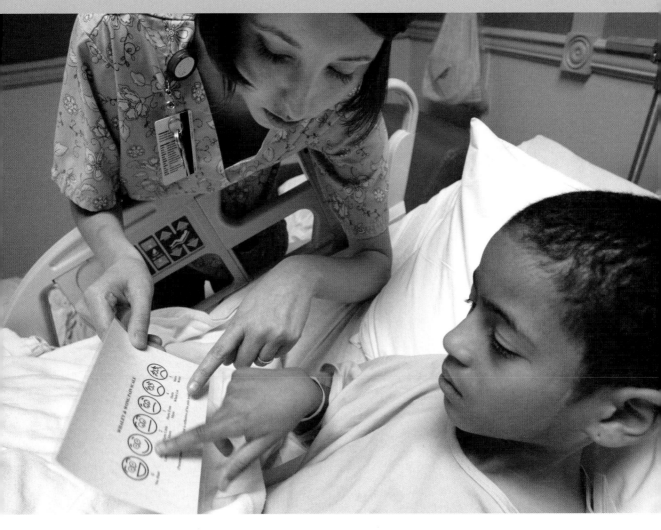

The pictures on the Wong-Baker pain scale are especially helpful to children.
They might find it more difficult than adults to describe the intensity of their pain.

Humans experience pain at all ages. We learn something valuable whenever we suffer pain: avoidance of situations that cause pain. However, sometimes pain finds us anyway if we get sick or accidentally injure ourselves.

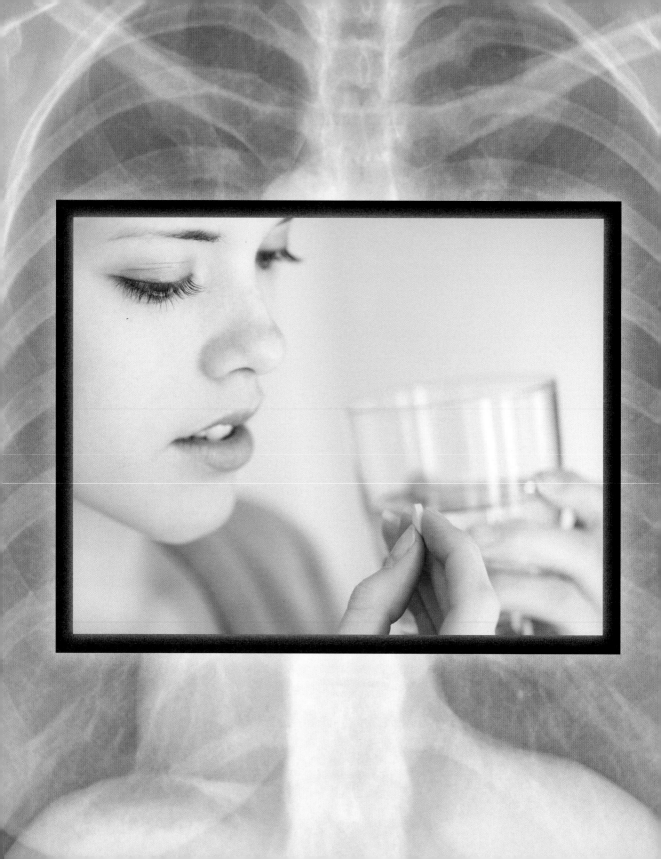

chapter 3

What Are Pain Medications?

Pain medications are the different medical **drugs** people take to stop pain. Like all drugs, pain medications are chemicals that change the brain. A painkiller might be as simple as an **ibuprofen** tablet to get rid of a headache. Or it might be a doctor's prescription for a combined painkiller and **antidepressant** to treat nerve pain.

Taking pain medications is just one of several ways to get relief while the body heals.

19

The Pain Reliever Within

The most common pain reliever is not found in a doctor's office, drugstore, first-aid kit, or medicine cabinet. Natural pain relievers are made right inside our own bodies whenever an injury or medical condition causes pain.

Researchers using brain-scanning machines have been able to see just how this natural pain reliever works. Pain specialists at the University of Michigan Dental School took brain images of a group of volunteers who agreed to undergo mild levels of jaw pain. About twenty minutes after the pain started, the volunteers' brains began to release natural painkilling chemicals into the central nervous system. These **endorphins** are the same chemicals that temporarily make us feel good when we exercise hard or have other kinds of intense physical experiences. Researchers observed the volunteers' "feel good" endorphins locking on to **opioid receptors** in their brains and spinal cords. Endorphin action temporarily slowed pain signals between the peripheral nervous system and the central nervous system. As a result, the volunteers reported less pain.

Pain expert Robert C. Coghill conducted a pain study sponsored by the U.S. National Institutes of Health in 2006. Coghill examined whether the pain people expected influenced the actual pain they felt. Researchers repeatedly caused three levels of heat pain in volunteers. However, sometimes volunteers actually received a different level of pain than what they were told. MRI images showed that if subjects expected to get a low level of pain but got a higher one, they reported low pain levels. This also happened the other way around.

Pain experts believe this occurs because people in pain use past experiences to form mental pictures of what they think will happen during a painful experience. From this experiment Coghill concluded that "pain needs to be treated with more than just pills. The brain can powerfully shape pain, and we need to exploit its power."

The Power of Expectations and Placebos

Pain experts now know that a patient's expectation of pain relief from a treatment can trigger endorphins in almost the same way that the sight of food can trigger the release of saliva. This is the reason **placebo**, or fake, treatments work for a short time. When someone expects that a fake pain-killer—a placebo—will work, this belief sets off the body's own **opioids**. This short-lived endorphin release slows down pain signals, bringing the patient temporary relief.

Unfortunately, the body's natural opioids only have temporary effects. Most medical drugs produce more lasting results. A drug's specific active ingredients—the chief chemicals that produce effects—usually continue working while the patient takes them.

Major Drug Pain Relievers

Since we have natural painkillers inside us, why would we need anything else? The answer is that the body's endorphins only work long enough to help people tend to their injuries. If the body produced too many endorphins, people might not take care of themselves right away.

Pain sufferers occasionally need more relief than the body's natural opi-oids can give them. That is when **analgesics** can come to the rescue. *Analgesic* comes from a Greek word that means "without pain." Analgesic painkillers include **aspirin**, ibuprofen, acetaminophen, **naproxen**, as well as stronger drugs, such as manufactured **opiates**, and more. Analgesics relieve pain in a couple of ways. All of them dull pain signals from the peripheral nervous system. Some of them also lower inflammation.

Pain sufferers can get analgesics in two ways. They can buy **over-the-counter (OTC) medications**, including pain relievers, from a drugstore or supermarket. Many people keep aspirin, ibuprofen, acetaminophen, or naproxen in their medicine cabinets and first-aid kits. These OTC pain-killers usually relieve everyday headaches, muscle aches, sprains, tooth-aches, and other pains.

OTC pain relievers may not be strong enough for the pain associated with recovery from surgery, a bone break, a flare-up of terrible arthritis joint pain, or other serious injuries. In such cases, pain sufferers can get stronger prescription painkillers from doctors.

The World Health Organization (WHO) pain ladder is a guide for medical professionals. Over-the-counter, low-side-effect drugs are offered first before more powerful, multiple-side-effect painkillers are prescribed.

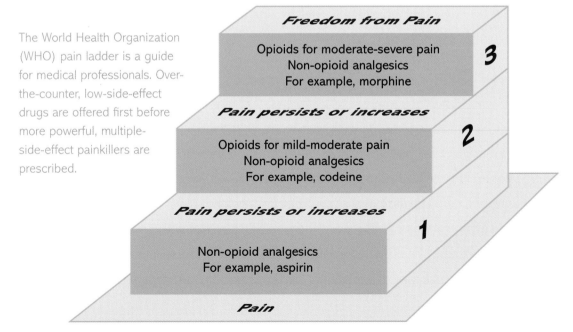

Freedom from Pain

Opioids for moderate-severe pain
Non-opioid analgesics
For example, morphine

3

Pain persists or increases

Opioids for mild-moderate pain
Non-opioid analgesics
For example, codeine

2

Pain persists or increases

Non-opioid analgesics
For example, aspirin

1

Pain

The doctor will ask the patient questions about the injury or infection. He or she will examine the patient and form an educated opinion, or **diagnosis**, about the cause of the pain. Before prescribing a pain reliever, the doctor will also ask about the patient's pain levels. A written prescription specifies the name of the medication, the quantity to take, and the schedule for taking it. A pharmacist at a drugstore prepares the medication and includes printed directions for taking it and warnings about possible side effects.

Doctors are careful to prescribe the lowest **dose** of any pain medication first. Some pain relievers interfere with other medications. Certain pain medications may cause some people to become dependent on them—they keep taking the drug after their pain has gone away. For these reasons doctors usually suggest the mildest painkillers they think will work. If these do not help the patient enough, the doctor may prescribe something stronger later on.

Nonsteroidal Anti-Inflammatory Drugs

Walk through any drugstore and it is hard to miss the dozens of pill bottles, liquid painkillers, and pain-relieving creams and gels. These colorful boxes and plastic bottles all look so different, yet most of them contain **nonsteroidal anti-inflammatory drugs**. That is the long name for NSAIDs, which include aspirin, ibuprofen, and naproxen. Despite the different packaging, these three major NSAIDs all have a couple of things in common: they dull pain signals and they affect the chemicals in cells that cause inflammation. This helps swelling to go down.

When an injury or medical condition starts, cells at the pain site quickly produce pain-causing prostaglandin. This excites nerve endings that send pain signals through the central nervous system. The person feels pain.

He or she takes one of the NSAIDs, and the following occurs:

- The NSAID dissolves in the stomach after it is swallowed.

- The NSAID enters the bloodstream and travels all over the body. At the injury site, the NSAID's active ingredient slows down prostaglandin production in the damaged cells.

- The prostaglandin slowdown means the brain does not receive fast, clear pain signals anymore. As a result, less pain is felt although the injured or irritated nerve endings are still sending pain signals.

- Tissue swelling starts to go down.

- All this pain-relieving activity can take anywhere from ten minutes to two hours, depending on the dose and the type of NSAID taken. With repeated doses, relief can last for hours or days until the injury heals.

Serious Side Effects of Over-the-Counter Pain Relievers

Any NSAID—aspirin, ibuprofen, or naproxen—should be taken for as short a time as possible. Each of them affects *all* prostaglandins in the body, not just pain-related ones. Some prostaglandins protect the stomach and the digestive system from acids that break down our food when we eat. Since NSAIDs reduce prostaglandin activity everywhere in the body, bleeding in the digestive system can be a serious side effect.

Acetaminophen is another commonly used painkiller. However, it does not affect inflammation. It comes with strong warning labels that should be

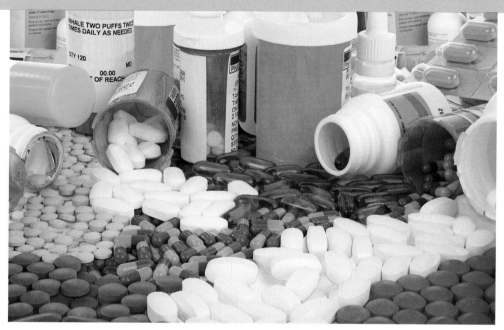

The many varieties of pain medications work by reducing swelling or dulling pain signals. All pain medications have some side effects, however.

read and followed very carefully. More people have died from acetaminophen poisoning than from any other over-the-counter drug. A 2010 *New York Times* article reported new findings that indicate that young teens who take acetaminophen at least once a month are twice as likely to develop asthma as teens who never take it. Some frequent teen users also experience eye, nose, and skin irritations. Acetaminophen has the potential to cause deadly liver damage if someone takes too much of it or takes it while drinking alcohol. Certain individuals suffer liver damage from acetaminophen without taking it in overdose levels or with alcohol. Anyone who takes acetaminophen should take it infrequently, in the lowest possible doses, and for the shortest possible time.

Anyone with diabetes, asthma, or allergies needs to check with a doctor about taking painkillers. Some people are allergic to acetylsalicylic acid, commonly known as aspirin. NSAIDs may also interfere with medications that diabetics take to control their condition.

Nerve-Pain Medications

Stabbing, pins and needles, burning, tingling, and numbness are just a few of the ways people with nerve damage describe their pain. Over a hundred different conditions can cause nerve damage. Just a few of them include accidental injuries, back pain, facial pain, severe coughing, surgical injuries, cancer, diabetes, and certain infections. Nerve injuries are among the most severe and longest lasting of all pains. The pain may come and go, but sufferers dread each episode. Nerve pain can be difficult to treat.

Doctors may prescribe different analgesic painkillers along with antidepressants. This combination helps quiet pain signals and calm emotional centers in the pain-brain network. Doctors treating nerve pain sometimes prescribe antiseizure drugs to lower nerve activity in the brain and spinal cord.

Opiates

You will not see boxes and bottles of opiates while walking down the aisles of a drugstore. That is because the U.S. government controls their use. It is against the law to obtain opiates for pain treatment without a doctor's prescription. All opiates have serious side effects. They greatly slow down the body's activities, such as breathing and heart rate. Opiates are habit-forming and can lead to drug dependence and addiction.

Like the body's own opioids, many drug opiates can be found in nature, specifically in the sap of the poppy flower. Some opiates are manufactured in synthetic, or artificial, forms as well.

The poppy flower, from which painkilling opium is harvested, has been used as a source of pain medications since ancient times. Poppies are grown legally for use in painkillers but illegally for use in heroin, an outlawed drug in most countries.

Whether natural or artificial, opiates such as **heroin**, codeine, morphine, and prescription painkillers mimic the brain's opioids. That is, they lock on to the brain's opioid receptors to dull or block pain signals. But the chemistry is a little different. The body's opioids release endorphins. Opiates trigger **dopamine** production. Dopamine arouses pleasure and reward centers in the brain. So opiates not only reduce pain signals, they also create a deep feeling of calm. In addition, they promote sleep, which is needed for healing. The calming, pain-blocking effects of opiates help relieve many types of intense pain due to surgical wounds, muscle injuries, broken bones, backaches, arthritis joint inflammation, uncontrollable coughing, cancer, or cancer treatments.

Some opiates, such as hydrocodone, are combined with acetaminophen in medications such as Vicodin and Lorcet. This combination is often more effective than either painkiller alone. However, since each opiate analgesic has separate, serious side effects, doctors supervise combined painkillers carefully.

Opiates come in pill form or in liquids that can be swallowed. They can also be administered as slow-drip vein injections—IVs—after surgery or extremely painful injuries. Liquid morphine is administered this way. Some opiates, such as Lidocaine, are given through needles and can block local pain signals. They are useful during dental procedures or when a wound needs stitching.

Opiates have many side effects. Some of them can be deadly. Negative side effects include:

- Reduced breathing and heart rate

- Digestive problems, such as constipation and nausea, since opiates cause natural opioids in the digestive system to become sluggish

- Allergic reactions and rashes

- **Depression** and mood swings due to a slowdown in emotional areas of the central nervous system

- Decreased reaction time, which is a danger when driving a vehicle

- Deafness with long-term use

- Opiate dependence and addiction

- Unconsciousness or death at overdose levels or with unsafe drug and alcohol combinations

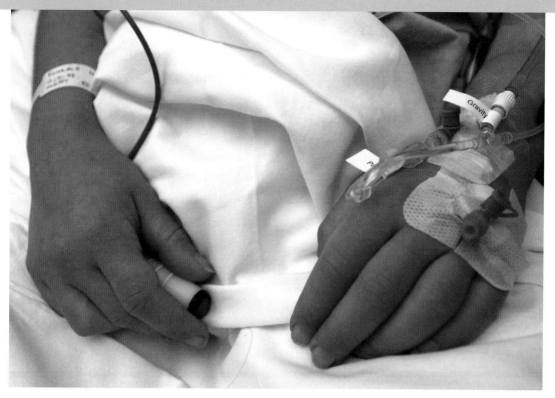

In the most difficult days after surgery, patients may use a morphine pump to deliver doses of the painkiller as they require it.

Illegal use of opiate prescription drugs has become a huge problem. Many opiate abusers believe these drugs are safe because a doctor prescribed them for someone. However, opiates are only approved in the doses prescribed for the person whose name is on the label. These drugs can be addictive and dangerous for anyone else. In 2008 illegal abuse of a single opiate, OxyContin, led to 105,000 visits to emergency rooms due to overdoses. Thousands of opiate-dependent drug users die from opiate poisoning each year.

Pain Medications at a Glance

Prescription Pain Relievers

Brand Name	Chemical Name & Active Ingredients	Best For	Side Effects*
OxyContin	opiate: oxycodone	surgical pain, serious muscle and skeletal pain, severe back pain	risk of Reye's syndrome in children and young adults; possible allergic reaction to acetylsalicylic acid
Percocet, Percodan	opiate: oxycodone (Percocet: oxycodone with acetaminophen) (Percodan: oxycodone with aspirin)	moderate to moderately severe surgical pain, muscle and skeletal pain, back pain, dental pain	risk of Reye's syndrome in children and young adults; risk of liver damage and death when misused at overdose levels or in combination with alcohol or other drugs
Vicodin, Lorcet	opiate: hydrocodone with acetaminophen	moderate to moderately severe surgical pain, muscle and skeletal pain, back pain, dental pain, intense coughing	drowsiness, rash, high blood pressure; long-term use increases risk of heart attack or stroke in older people
Tylenol with Codeine, Capital and Codeine, Brontex, and others	opiate: codeine	coughing, moderate pain	constipation, shortness of breath; long-term use increases risk of heart attack or stroke in older people
Dilaudid, Palladone	opiate: dihydromorphinone	severe pain in certain patients (not as commonly used as other pain medications)	decreased heart and breathing rates, constipation, drowsiness, drug dependence
Avinza, Kadian, MS Contin, MSIR, Oramorph SR, Roxanol	opiate: morphine and methylmorphine	agonizing pain from surgery, cancer, severe injuries, severe back pain, kidney stones, severe diarrhea, severe coughing	decreased heart and breathing rates, constipation, drowsiness, hearing loss, drug dependence, coma, death

Over-the-Counter Pain Relievers

Brand Name	Chemical Name & Active Ingredients	Best For	Side Effects*
Anacin, Bayer Aspirin, Bufferin	aspirin, acetylsalicylic acid	mild headaches, muscle aches	risk of Reye's syndrome in children and young adults; possible allergic reaction to acetylsalicylic acid
Excedrin, Tylenol	acetaminophen, aspirin, caffeine	fever, colds, flu, arthritis joint pain, bone and muscle pain	risk of Reye's syndrome in children and young adults; risk of liver damage and death when misused at overdose levels or in combination with alcohol or other drugs
Advil, Motrin, Nuprin	ibuprofen	fever, backache, headache, muscle aches, tissue swelling	drowsiness, rash, high blood pressure; long-term use increases risk of heart attack or stroke in older people
Aleve, Naproxen	naproxen sodium	arthritis joint pain, muscle and bone pain, menstrual cramps, tissue swelling	constipation, shortness of breath; long-term use increases risk of heart attack or stroke in older people

*Note: Stomachache, stomach bleeding, and aggravation of existing ulcers are potential side effects of all painkillers. Listed side effects reflect a partial list.

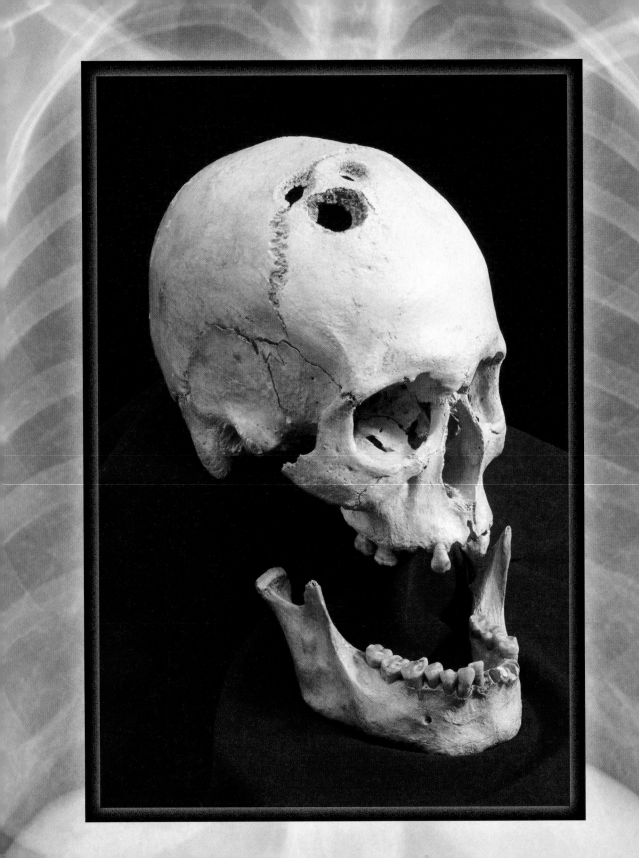

chapter 4

History of Pain Treatments

The mummified body had been lying in the ice-covered Italian Alps for about 5,300 years when two tourists discovered it in 1991. Thick ice had preserved the man's tissues, bones, and teeth for all that time. Later, X-rays and other imaging techniques showed that the man had suffered many injuries during his lifetime, including a head injury. He seems to have died from an arrowhead wound to his shoulder. Marks on his fingernails indicated that he had suffered several infections in the year before he died.

◄ This skull, discovered in the city of Jericho in Palestine, shows evidence of an ancient pain treatment: medical practitioners drilled holes into a patient's head to relieve pressure, ease pain and, perhaps, release troublesome spirits.

Archaeologists (scientists who study past human life) have found other ancient mummies and skeletons around the world. The bones show scarring from fractures, animal tooth marks, and arrowheads. Some preserved tissues indicate diseases such as arthritis and tuberculosis, from which people still suffer today.

Unlike today, though, prehistoric and ancient humans in pain did not have modern painkillers to relieve their suffering. No wonder the ancient Greeks blamed their pains on the goddess of revenge, Poena. They believed that she punished people with physical suffering if they angered the gods. The word *pain* comes from her name. Several hundred years later, the religious figure Saint Augustine (354–430 CE) said, "The greatest evil is physical pain."

What did people do to relieve this "greatest evil" before there were opiates, aspirin, and shelves of other painkillers? They probably suffered more than people do today. Yet archaeologists and historians have found evidence going back to prehistoric times that humans had searched for pain relief just as humans do now. Ancient peoples turned to prayers, ceremonies, special tools, and plant-based remedies to rid themselves of pain. Some of these treatments may seem crude, but a number of them were the forerunners of today's pain-relieving methods.

Many early treatments for pain involved reducing the pressure caused by inflammation. These methods included cutting, puncturing, or drilling into bones or the skull—a procedure called trepanation. Archaeologists digging in South America, France, and Germany have found many prehistoric skulls drilled with small holes. This painful treatment would have triggered the release of the body's own painkilling endorphins for temporary relief.

To this day, some trepanation techniques are used to relieve pressure in different parts of the body, including the skull.

Acupuncture, which has existed since before 2500 BCE, is an ancient pain treatment that may have been related to trepanation. However, fine needles, not drills, were placed on the body at different points to relieve pain. Ancient acupuncturists thought that needling affected special energies in the body. Today's pain specialists can now look inside the brain to see how acupuncture actually affects it. Researchers in a 1999 study said acupuncture needles triggered endorphin production so that research subjects felt temporary pain relief. A different study, on which the *New York Times*

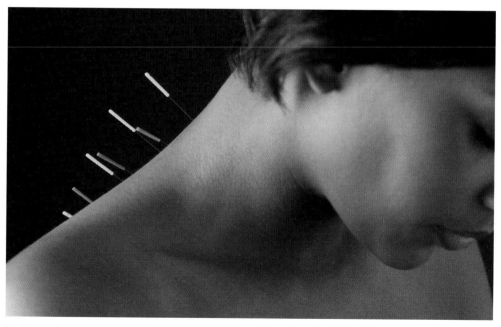

In 2010 the journal *Arthritis Care and Research* reported that fake acupuncture relieved pain as well as traditional acupuncture, probably because in both cases patients' expectations of relief triggered the body's natural pain-relieving endorphins.

reported in 2010, found, "Fake acupuncture appears to work just as well for pain relief as the real thing" in patients suffering from arthritis knee pain. Another 2010 study, at the University of York in England, found that acupuncture affected pain-processing structures of the brain.

Other ancient medical practitioners used mild electrical currents to treat pain. They knew that common eels, certain catfish, and torpedo fish gave off electrical charges, which caused numbness when these fish bit swimmers. So using the fish to cause numbness seemed a possible way to interrupt pain. One Greek medical practitioner, Claudius Galen (131–201 CE),

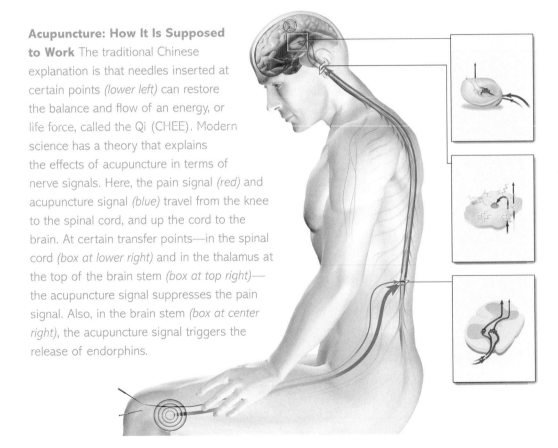

Acupuncture: How It Is Supposed to Work The traditional Chinese explanation is that needles inserted at certain points *(lower left)* can restore the balance and flow of an energy, or life force, called the Qi (CHEE). Modern science has a theory that explains the effects of acupuncture in terms of nerve signals. Here, the pain signal *(red)* and acupuncture signal *(blue)* travel from the knee to the spinal cord, and up the cord to the brain. At certain transfer points—in the spinal cord *(box at lower right)* and in the thalamus at the top of the brain stem *(box at top right)*—the acupuncture signal suppresses the pain signal. Also, in the brain stem *(box at center right)*, the acupuncture signal triggers the release of endorphins.

wrote: "The sea torpedo is said by some to cure headache. . . . The torpedo should be applied alive to the person who has the headache."

Later, in the 1800s, electrical shock anesthesia was used in amputation surgeries. Since 1967 electrical devices have been implanted in thousands of people who suffer from chronic pain. The devices give off electrical charges that stimulate nerves in the peripheral nervous system. When it works, this stimulation seems to disrupt some pain signals traveling along the nerve pathways of people suffering from chronic pain. So maybe those ancient Greeks were on to something when they advised taking a live, electrically charged fish and applying it to the forehead!

In prehistoric times, knowledge of medicinal plants was passed on orally from one generation to the next. This knowledge later became part of written records. The father of modern medicine, the Greek doctor Hippocrates (460-370 BCE), left behind notes recommending the use of willow bark powder to cure headaches and lower fevers. That centuries-old pain reliever turned out to be an early version of one of the most common pain relievers we use today: none other than ordinary aspirin! When it comes to painkillers, 95 percent of them today are based on aspirin or **opium**, which were both originally derived from plants.

Opium is made from the dried, concentrated sap of the poppy flower. Images of poppies appear on Sumerian objects that are more than six thousand years old. Opium is mentioned in many ancient medical writings. It has been a major pain reliever and surgical drug for thousands of years.

Medical use of opium became widespread after 1804 when a German scientist, Friedrich Sertürner, separated out the opium poppy's active ingredient, morphine. This was soon available for sale all over the world, until

Time Line of Pain Treatments

3500 BCE Poppies are grown in Mesopotamia; opium is made from their dried sap.

3000 BCE Sumerian medical stone tablets list willow bark, the plant source of aspirin, as a remedy.

3000–2500 BCE Egyptian medical scrolls mention opium being used to treat pain and as anesthesia in surgery.

460–370 BCE Greek doctor Hippocrates recommends willow bark to ease childbirth pain.

100 BCE Acupuncture procedures that had been practiced for centuries are described in *The Yellow Emperor's Classic of Internal Medicine.*

46 BCE Greek medical practitioner Dioscorides applies electricity from live, electrically charged torpedo fish to relieve headaches.

500–1500 CE Live leech therapy is regularly used to relieve pain and inflammation.

1537 European medical literature notes reintroduction of opium in a painkilling pill called laudanum.

1804 German chemist Friedrich Sertürner discovers opium's active ingredient, morphine.

doctors realized something terrible about this miracle painkiller: it is extremely addictive. Drug researchers continued searching for another major miracle drug to treat pain and discovered heroin. This chemical is made from morphine. As the world knows now, heroin is even more addictive than morphine. Both opium-derived drugs have been under

1838 Italian chemist Raffaele Piria develops a powerful extract of salicylic acid from willow bark.

1894 The Bayer Company in Germany manufactures the first aspirin from salicylic acid.

1895 The Bayer Company in Germany refines morphine into heroin for medical use.

1914 The United States passes the Harrison Narcotics Act, requiring doctors and pharmacists to register with the government to prescribe opium-based drugs due to widespread morphine and heroin addiction.

1916–1920 Oxycodone and hydrocodone are chemically created in Germany from opium as alternatives to morphine and heroin.

mid–1940s First pain clinics founded in the United States.

1953 Acetaminophen first marketed in the United States.

1950s Professor Tsung-Ying Shen discovers the first nonsteroidal anti-inflammatory drugs.

1974 Ibuprofen developed in England and introduced in the United States.

1979 The use of epidural opioid injections into the spine begins.

2010 Researchers work on a new generation of non-opioid painkillers that use the same receptors in the body that detect heat from chili peppers.

government control in most places around the world since the early 1900s.

The search for safe, reliable pain treatments continues. Now that pain experts can see detailed brain images of what happens during pain, they are on the hunt for targeted treatments. Someday, new painkillers will go straight to the injury instead of traveling through the whole body.

chapter 5

Pain Prevention and Treatments

Accidents happen. Sooner or later, everyone gets scraped or bruised. Students often stay up too late on the weekends and wake up with headaches when it is time to go back to school. During certain times of the year, it seems as if everyone in a classroom is coughing, sniffling, or feeling achy. Some people are born with painful conditions such as cerebral palsy, or they develop painful conditions such as juvenile rheumatoid arthritis.

◄ Every day, emergency rooms in the United States receive thousands of children and adults with sports injuries. The use of proper equipment, such as helmets, knee pads, elbow protectors, and shin guards, can prevent many painful injuries.

Being alive, active, and around other people means there is always a risk of injury, infection, and pain. But there are many good habits that can help prevent injuries, infections, and the pain they cause.

- Always, 100 percent of the time, wear a seat belt when riding in a car.

- Wear a bike helmet and learn the rules of safe biking.

- Learn the rules of safe walking and jogging on roads. Wear bright clothes, walk or run facing traffic, and avoid using earbuds or headphones so you can hear cars coming.

- Wear the recommended protective gear for whatever sport you do.

- When a coach or gym teacher advises you to get in shape before your sports season, get in shape before your sports season! Many athletes injure muscles, knees, shoulders, and ligaments because they ignore the advice to slowly build up their exercise program if they have been inactive for a while.

- Do not hike in the wilderness without a buddy, a map, a first-aid kit, and food and water. Always tell someone your route and expected return time.

- Wear sunscreen, insect repellent, and long pants if you go into areas with a lot of ticks or mosquitoes.

- Drink plenty of water every day. Many headaches are caused by dehydration.

- Get nine to ten hours of sleep every night and try to go to bed at the same time every night. Cell repair goes on during sleep. Being overtired is a risk factor for accidents.

- Eat energy-building foods such as fruits, veggies, whole grains, dairy or soy products (including milk, yogurt, and cheese), and proteins—beans, nuts, or small amounts of meat, chicken, or eggs.

- Find some form of exercise you enjoy even if it is not a team sport. Exercise helps improve your balance, and it builds up the heart, muscles, and immune system.

- Wash your hands a lot—especially after being with groups of people, after going to the bathroom, and before eating.

- If food has been sitting out in a warm place for a long time, looks weird, or smells funny, pass it by.

- Is it safe? Is it smart? Is it legal? If something someone wants you to try is not safe, smart, or legal, memorize this answer: "No thanks."

- Listen to your body. It wants you to stop and take care of yourself if you do get sick or injured.

Taking all these precautions seriously puts the safety odds in your favor. However, it does not guarantee that you will never get hurt and need pain treatment. But before you head for the medicine cabinet, there is one remedy you can try first: self-help. It is the easiest, cheapest, most available pain treatment around.

Past pain experiences teach many people how to take care of most everyday injuries or illnesses. They may remember that their last neck ache went away after they took a break from the computer for a few days. Someone with stomach cramps may remember that lying down with a warm heating

RICE for Pain Relief

Pain-related RICE is not the white, sticky grain that comes with Chinese takeout. It is a proven method for healing bruises, sprains, broken bones, pulled muscles, and those aches we all get once in a while even if we do follow all the safety rules.

RICE stands for Rest, Ice, Compression, Elevation. Here is how to follow this great healing first-aid method:

Rest the injured body part right away.

Ice the injured body part with something cold—ice in a plastic bag or a towel, or one of those blue-gel cold packs. Even a bag of frozen veggies can help! Ice the damaged tissues as soon as possible. Continue icing for a few days for periods of thirty minutes on and thirty minutes off during the time you are awake. Protect your skin from freezer burn by wrapping your ice or cold pack in a soft cloth or towel.

Compress the injured body part by wrapping it protectively. Those tan elastic bandages work well for compression. They should be wrapped so that they are tight enough to reduce blood flow but not so tight that they stop blood flow.

Elevate that body part so that blood goes toward the heart in order to reduce the swelling. Reduced inflammation lessens pain.

Very often, RICE is the only treatment an injury needs. If you still hurt, take ibuprofen or naproxen under a grown-up's supervision and as directed on the bottle.

pad on the stomach helped a lot. The human body is often the best healer because it produces those great painkilling endorphins on its own without side effects.

First Aid Starts at Home

Healing most everyday pains requires a visit to the first-aid kit, not the doctor. That is because your body has its own endorphins to make you feel well enough to take care of yourself. A basic first-aid kit needs a few simple supplies to help you care for a cut, bruise, headache, toothache, sunburn, or sliver. Supplies to keep in a first-aid box or bag should include: emergency phone numbers, different-sized bandages, antibiotic ointment, an elastic bandage, tweezers, adhesive tape and nonstick bandages for bigger cuts or

Ice packs are one of the best treatments for swelling right after an injury. And you don't need a prescription for them!

wounds, antiseptic wipes, and small scissors. Keep two soft gel packs in the freezer. Most families keep a thermometer plus aspirin, ibuprofen, or other over-the-counter NSAIDs on hand.

Use the RICE method for sprains, bruises, and possible fractures. When you get injured, always inform an adult in case more treatment is needed than you can do at home. Earaches, sore throats, rashes, fevers, and severe stomach pains may need medical attention.

What to Do for an Ordinary Headache

When a headache starts to build, stop what you are doing if you can. Wet a washcloth, wring it out, and stick it in the freezer. If you skipped a meal or have not drunk any liquids for a while, have a small, healthy snack and drink a couple of glasses of water. Your hunger or thirst might be causing your headache. Your parent may suggest taking ibuprofen. Take the washcloth from the freezer. Go lie down. Put the cool washcloth on your forehead. Over-tiredness and mixed-up sleep schedules cause many headaches. Take a nap.

What to Do for Cuts, Scrapes, and Wound Pains

If you get a cut, a scrape, or any other injury that breaks the skin, stop what you are doing. Check with an adult to see if the injury needs stitches at the doctor's office or the emergency room. If not, get a clean cloth, antiseptic wipe, or clean tissue. Press it over the wound for fifteen minutes or so to stop the bleeding. If you have a cold pack in the freezer, hold it over the cloth to decrease inflammation. Wash the cut with soap and water and dry it with a clean tissue or towel. Apply antiseptic cream or gel to the injury. Apply a

Band-Aid or a bandage to it. Change the bandage if it gets dirty. After a scab forms, let the cut or wound air out. Put antiseptic cream on it until it heals so it does not get infected. If it does become infected, see a doctor.

What to Do about Stomach and Menstrual Pains

Pain specialists have found that gentle warmth from a heating pad or hot-water bottle activates heat receptors in the abdominal area that slow down chemical pain signals to the brain. Warmth sometimes stops the pain completely.

What to Do about Chronic or Serious Pain

Serious acute pain as well as chronic pain are not conditions a person can fix with a cool cloth or first aid. Family members, friends, and especially medical professionals can help with organizing a pain treatment plan for people who have permanent injuries or conditions.

Pain specialists usually suggest several actions for dealing with serious or ongoing pain. The patient should acknowledge that he or she is experiencing pain that needs treatment. He or she should also follow medical recommendations for fixing the cause of the pain if that is possible.

Many people in pain learn to distract themselves with activities they can do even if they are in pain: a hobby, listening to music, watching funny movies—anything that gets the brain distracted. In one major pain distraction study conducted in the late 1990s, virtual reality software developers came to the rescue of burn patients undergoing extremely painful procedures while they healed. The developers created "SnowWorld," a game that the burn patients could play with the use of special helmets and goggles.

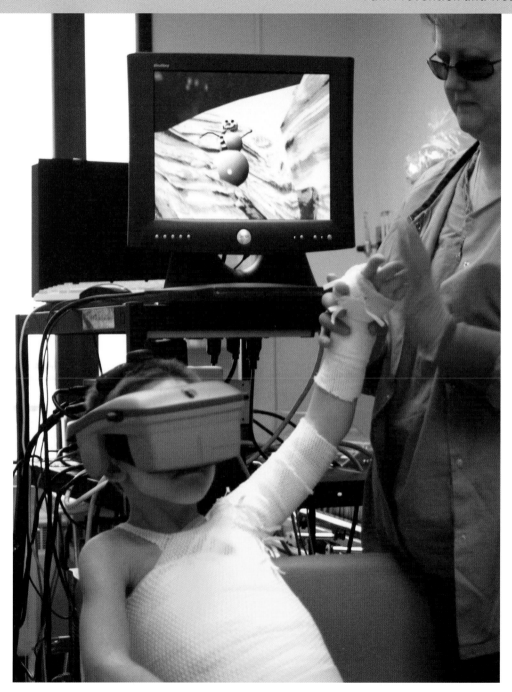

This snowy virtual reality game is helping a young burn victim distract himself from pain.

During the game players shot virtual snowballs at robots and penguins, and they traveled through icy lands. The game reduced pain perception by as much as 90 percent!

Research shows that **psychological** therapy can help some people in chronic pain to break the negative mental cycle of thinking that their conditions may never improve. Deep massage under medical supervision can reduce chronic pain sufferers' pain perception. So can floating in a float pool or doing gentle swimming.

People in pain need to find a balance between rest and movement. More and more doctors recommend exercise programs for conditions such as backaches that used to keep people in bed. One well-known pain specialist, Vijay Vad of the New York Hospital for Special Surgery, works to keep patients *out* of surgery! For people with chronic back pain, joint pains, and overall general chronic pain, Vad recommends thirty minutes a day of gentle exercise, which releases endorphins and quiets pain signals. According to Vad, "You become pain desensitized by proper exercise with gradual increases in stress."

People in pain should encourage others to treat them as healthy people having a temporary physical setback.

What Are the Alternatives?

Self-help and the body's own healing powers are often the best alternative pain treatments to medication that you can give yourself. After taking care of your injury, you will wake up one day and find that your sprained ankle does not hurt or that your burn is all better.

Some people prefer not to take any OTC or prescribed drugs. They turn to nonmedical therapies, such as acupuncture, **chiropractic**, **homeopathy**,

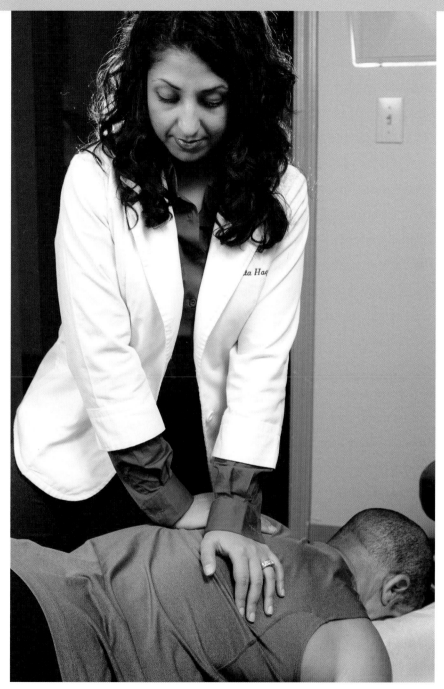

Therapeutic massage not only helps trigger the brain's release of endorphins, it may also help heal injured cells.

or other nondrug treatments. Many of these treatments have been around for hundreds, even thousands, of years.

The difference between alternative therapies and medical ones is that medical treatments have undergone rigorous, repeatable scientific tests that have produced the same results each time. Aspirin was once an alternative treatment until repeated testing showed that its active ingredient worked to lower prostaglandin pain signals.

Because pain always triggers some endorphin release, the body itself produces its own painkillers after an injury. New cells replace injured ones. Infectious germs and viruses are killed. The patient gets better. If he or she happened to get an acupuncture treatment or tried an alternative healing substance, how could it be determined whether those remedies worked or the condition got better on its own?

Answering such questions is one aim of The Cochrane Collaboration. Founded in 1993, this voluntary group of about 28,000 international medical professionals gathers the most well-organized, evidence-based medical studies from all over the world. They report on whether or not certain mainstream or alternative methods and drugs work. The Cochrane Collaboration has pulled together many studies on pain treatments, such as acupuncture and chiropractic. Millions of people try these alternative treatments instead of standard medical drug treatments or in addition to them.

The Cochrane Collaboration found positive news for people who get repeated, severe tension headaches. Combined headache studies show that people who followed basic headache treatments, plus acupuncture, reported about 90 percent fewer headaches than headache sufferers who followed just basic headache treatments: over-the-counter or prescription headache medications. However, most acupuncture treatments for other conditions simply set off temporary placebo effects.

Lower-back pain is one of the most common and expensive medical conditions to treat. Those who suffer from it sometimes try many treatments to ease this pain, including surgery. One nonsurgical treatment is spinal manipulation with a chiropractor. The Cochrane Collaboration concluded from twelve major studies that chiropractic spinal manipulation did not significantly relieve lower back pain. According to the National Pain Foundation, 90 percent of back pain will decrease on its own.

Homeopathy is a popular treatment for various ailments and pains. Homeopathy uses highly watered-down substances that would cause illness if someone took them at full strength. The thinking is that the diluted form will strengthen the body to fight back. Many well-designed major studies on homeopathy have been done. All of them conclude that homeopathy has no therapeutic value beyond a placebo effect. That may be enough for the many people who believe in homeopathy and expect it to help.

When pain does strike, the best alternative treatment of all may be your thoughts. As pain expert Robert C. Coghill points out, "Our data shows that what you *think* really changes what you *experience*."

Glossary

acetaminophen A common pain reliever and fever reducer that can be obtained without a doctor's prescription.

acupuncture An ancient treatment using needles to block pain signals.

acute pain Sudden, sharp, intense pain.

analgesics Painkilling medications that slow down pain signals.

anesthesia Medications that dull pain, numb it completely, or cause someone to become unconscious.

antidepressant Medication that lifts negative moods.

arthritis A medical condition that causes painful joints.

aspirin A pain reliever, originally made from willow bark, that also reduces swelling and lowers fever; a nonsteroidal anti-inflammatory drug.

central nervous system (CNS) The system of nerves in the brain and spinal cord.

chiropractic A method of healing muscular and skeletal pain by manipulating the body's posture.

chronic pain A continuing feeling of discomfort after an injury has healed, after a stimulus has stopped, or due to an incurable condition.

codeine A natural painkiller found in poppy flowers; used to treat pain either alone or in combination with other medications.

dehydration A dangerous lack of necessary fluids in the body.

depression Ongoing feelings of deep unhappiness.

diagnosis A doctor's medical opinion about a condition.

dopamine A brain chemical that carries messages to other cells and triggers pleasurable feelings.

dose The recommended amount of a drug to be taken.

drugs Chemical substances that cause changes in the brain.

endorphins Pain-relieving, calming chemicals that the body releases under pain and stress.

genes Inherited characteristics that are passed on from parents to offspring.

heroin A highly addictive pain-relieving drug that is made from poppies and that produces great calm and drowsiness.

homeopathy A nonmedical disease- and pain-treatment method.

ibuprofen An over-the-counter pain reliever that blocks pain signals and reduces swelling; a nonsteroidal anti-inflammatory drug.

infection The condition of having harmful agents in the body, such as germs or viruses.

inflammation The swelling, tenderness, and redness of tissues due to injury.

morphine A calming but highly addictive painkiller made from opium.

MRI (magnetic resonance imaging) A technique, similar to a CAT scan or an X-ray, that uses a strong magnetic field to produce an image of the inside of the body, especially of the brain, muscles and bones, the heart, and cancerous tumors.

naproxen A pain reliever that also reduces swelling and that can be obtained without a doctor's prescription; a nonsteroidal anti-inflammatory drug.

nerve cells Tiny bundles of fibers that exchange chemical and electrical messages with the brain.

neurotransmitters Nerve cell chemicals that send messages to activate other cells.

nociceptors Nerve endings in cells that respond to potentially damaging stimuli, the causes of an injury or infection.

nonsteroidal anti-inflammatory drugs Painkilling medications that lessen the swelling of injured blood vessels; also called NSAIDs.

opiates Manufactured drugs such as morphine, heroin, and other painkillers that contain chemicals made from the poppy flower or that mimic them.

opioid receptors Chemical particles in cells to which opioids and opiates attach.

opioids Natural chemicals, such as endorphins, that the body produces to temporarily dull pain signals.

opium A substance in the poppy flower that is used to make morphine, heroin, or manufactured opioids.

over-the-counter (OTC) medications Medications someone can buy in a drugstore or supermarket without a doctor's prescription.

pain The unpleasant physical and emotional feelings that result from injury to the body.

peripheral nervous system (PNS) A network of nerve pathways that sends messages to the brain about the body's condition.

physical therapy A treatment to help individuals lessen their pain and regain movement or use of their injured body part.

placebo A fake treatment that often brings about relief anyway.

prostaglandin A chemical substance that cells produce to control many functions, including pain.

psychological Relating to the mind.

receptors The points on a cell where drug chemicals or neurotransmitters attach.

spinal cord The long tube of nerve tissue, protected by bone, that extends from the brain and that carries pain and other messages.

tissues Groups of cells that carry out the same job.

Find Out More

Books

Culbert, Timothy, M.D. *Be the Boss of Your Pain: Self Care for Kids.* Minneapolis, MN: Free Spirit Publishing, 2007.

Krane, Elliot J., M.D., and Deborah Mitchell. *Relieve Your Child's Chronic Pain: A Doctor's Program for Easing Headaches, Abdominal Pain, Fibromyalgia, Juvenile Rheumatoid Arthritis, and More.* New York: Fireside, Simon and Schuster, 2005.

Lehman, Thomas J. A., M.D. *It's Not Just Growing Pains: A Guide to Childhood Muscle, Bone and Joint Pain, Rheumatic Diseases, and the Latest Treatments.* New York: Oxford University Press, 2004.

Olive, M. Foster. *Prescription Pain Relievers: Drugs, the Straight Facts.* New York: Chelsea House, 2005.

Singh, Simon, and Edzard Ernst, M.D. *Trick or Treatment.* New York: W. W. Norton, 2008.

Websites

Kids Health

http://kidshealth.org/kid/ill_injure/index.html

Kids Health is an easy-to-use website that provides useful medical information for children, teens, and their parents.

Massachusetts General Hospital

www.massachusettsgeneralhospital.org/children/patientsandfamilies/default.aspx

Massachusetts General Hospital is a major medical center with a highly regarded pain treatment department. Part of the hospital's website is dedicated to providing information, including advice about pain, to patients and their families.

National Pain Foundation

www.nationalpainfoundation.org

The mission of the National Pain Foundation is: "To improve the quality of life for those living with pain through information, education, and support that connects persons with pain to each other and to those that can help."

Organizations

American Pain Society

4700 West Lake Avenue

Glenview, IL 60025

Phone: 847-375-4715

Email: info@ampainsoc.org

www.ampainsoc.org

National Pain Foundation

300 East Hampden Avenue, Suite 100

Englewood, CO 80113

www.nationalpainfoundation.org

U.S. Cochrane Center

University of California

Suite 420

3333 California Street

San Francisco, CA 94118

Phone: 415-476-4958

www.cochrane.org

Index

Page numbers in **boldface** are illustrations.

About the Author

L. H. Colligan writes about many topics, from study skills to activity books, children's fiction to science and health nonfiction. She gained firsthand pain experience just before starting this book when she broke her arm on a winter hike. Two days of opiates helped her sleep through the worst of the early pain. After that, a week of ibuprofen once a day followed by six weeks of physical therapy and exercise helped her regain the use of her arm. She lives in western Massachusetts, where she is out hiking again.